blanks™

IC FELINES™

paperblanks™
FANTASTIC FELINES™

Blue Cats & Butterflies™

Laurel Burch is a self-taught artist and "flower child" living in California. In the 1960s, she sold handmade jewelry on the streets of San Francisco. Today, she continues to rely on her intuition and passion to create vibrant images of whimsy and allure with paint and paper. Brilliantly colored and exquisitely embellished with gold and silver, Fantastic Felines™ is one such theme portrayed on our journal covers—a visual flirtation with the seductive enigma that is the cat.

Laurel Buch, artiste autodidacte issue de la génération hyppie, vit en Californie. Dans les années 60, elle vendait ses bijoux dans les rues de san francisco. Aujourd'hui, forte de ce tempérament intuitif et créateur qui est le sien, elle poursuit son travail artistique avec une vitalité créatrice étonnante. Témoignant de son amour pour la vie, elle peint et dessine des sujets joyeusement colorés, illuminés d'or et d'argent. En couverture de nos carnets, voici des chats auréolés de mystère.

Laurel Burch es una artista autodidacta, hija de la generación hippy, en la actualidad residente en California. Ya en los años sesenta se dedicaba a la venta de joyería artesanal en las calles de San Francisco. Hoy en día sigue confiando en su intuición para expresar el leguaje del corazón con un estilo inconfundible que manifiesta su amor por la vida y su naturaleza fuertemente creativa. De su fértil imaginación crea con papel y pintura temas brillantemente coloreados, vibrantes y conmovedores, exquisitamente embellecidos con oro y plata. Felinos Fantásticos™ es uno de estos temas que presentamos en las cubiertas de nuestras agendas; una aventura visual con el seductor enigma del gato.

Laurel Burch, artista autodidatta e "figlia dei fiori" residente in California, negli anni '60 vendeva bigiotteria fatta a mano per le strade di San Francisco. Oggi, continuando ad affidarsi al proprio intuito e alla propria passione, crea con carta e colore immagini vivaci e capricciose. Fantastic Felines™ è uno dei soggetti, variopinti e squisitamente lumeggiati d'oro e d'argento, che abbiamo scelto per le nostre copertine: un flirt visivo con quell'affascinante enigma chiamato gatto.

Het "bloemenkind", de autodidactische kunstenares, Laurel Burch woont in Californië. In de zestiger jaren verkocht ze handgemaakte sieraden in de straten van San Francisco. Tegenwoordig gebruikt zij haar intuitie en passie om zeer levendige, eigenzinnige werken op papier te maken. De omslagen van deze serie cahiers Fantastic Felines™ is daareen voorbeeld van. Prachtig van kleur en rijkelijk versierd met goud en zilver is het een visuele flirt met het fenomeen de kat.

Laurel Burch hat in den 60er-Jahren als Blumenkind ihren selbst gemachten Schmuck auf den Straßen von San Francisco verkauft. Eine akademische Ausbildung hat die Kalifornierin bis heute nicht genossen. Sie verläßt sich lieber auf ihre Intuition und Leidenschaft: Daraus schöpft sie Inspiration und Mut zur Farbe auf Papier. In leuchtenden Farben, aufwändig verziert mit Gold und Silber, ist diese Reihe unseren Samtpfoten gewidmet. Sie sind schön und rätselhaft, eben Fantastic Felines™.

1-800-277-5887 (North America)
0 800-277-5887 (Germany)
0 800-328-4570 (UK)
Made in China.

www.paperblanks.com

ISBN 1-55156-466-1   160 PAGES   UNLINED